MEDITE
FREEZER MEALS
COOKBOOK

**"Over 50 Nutritious, Easy and Healthy
Make-Ahead Recipes to Improve
Wellness"**

Dayna G. Murphy

<u>GAIN ACCESS TO OTHER BOOKS BY ME</u>

TABLE OF CONTENTS

INTRODUCTION

Welcome and Introduction to Freezer Meals

Opening Statement:

Welcome to the world of convenient and delicious dining with the **"Mediterranean Freezer Meals Cookbook."** In this culinary adventure, we'll explore the vibrant and healthful flavors of the Mediterranean while embracing the ease and efficiency of freezer meals.

Captivating Introduction:

Imagine a kitchen where the rich aromas of garlic, olive oil, and fresh herbs fill the air, all while simplifying your daily meal preparations. The secret? Freezer meals inspired by the time-tested traditions of the Mediterranean. Whether you're a busy professional, a parent juggling multiple responsibilities or simply someone seeking a convenient way to enjoy exquisite cuisine, this cookbook is your ticket to a stress-free and flavorsome culinary experience.

Benefits of Freezer Meals

Time-Saving Magic:

Discover the magic of freezer meals, where a little upfront preparation leads to a bounty of ready-to-eat delights. Say goodbye to hectic weeknight dinners and embrace the luxury of having homemade Mediterranean feasts at your fingertips.

Budget-Friendly Brilliance:

Freezer meals are not only a time-saver but also a savvy financial choice. By buying ingredients in bulk and efficiently utilizing your kitchen resources, you'll find yourself spending less at the grocery store while still enjoying gourmet Mediterranean dishes.

Reducing Food Waste:

Worried about unused ingredients going to waste? With freezer meals, you can say farewell to spoilage and extend the life of fresh produce, ensuring every ingredient is put to good use. It's an eco-friendly way to savor the goodness of the Mediterranean while minimizing your environmental footprint.

How to Use This Cookbook

Your Culinary Guide:

This cookbook is designed to be your go-to resource for creating scrumptious Mediterranean freezer meals. Whether you're a seasoned chef or a kitchen novice, the user-friendly layout and detailed instructions will guide you through each step of the process.

Navigating the Chapters:

Begin your culinary journey with an exploration of the Mediterranean diet in Chapter 1. Then, dive into the practical aspects of freezer meal preparation in Chapter 2, and learn the art of planning and prepping in Chapter 3. The subsequent chapters will tantalize your taste buds with appetizers, main courses, vegetarian delights, side dishes, sauces, and sweet treats.

Pro Tips and Tricks:

Throughout the cookbook, you'll find pro tips, cooking hacks, and personal anecdotes to enhance your cooking experience. Whether it's advice on batch cooking or suggestions for refreshing flavors after freezing, these insights will empower you to create meals that are not only convenient but also bursting with authentic Mediterranean taste.

Embark on this culinary adventure with enthusiasm and confidence. The **"Mediterranean Freezer Meals Cookbook"** is your key to unlocking the joys of stress-free, flavorful dining. Let the journey begin!

CHAPTER 1: THE MEDITERRANEAN CUISINE

Overview of Mediterranean Diet

Introduction:

Delve into the heart of Mediterranean living by exploring the foundational principles of the Mediterranean diet. More than just a way of eating, it's a lifestyle that has captivated the world with its balance, variety, and emphasis on fresh, wholesome ingredients.

Foundational Elements:

- Abundance of Fresh Fruits and Vegetables
- Whole Grains as Staple Foods
- Lean Proteins, Primarily Fish and Poultry
- Healthy Fats from Olive Oil and Nuts
- Moderate Consumption of Dairy, Mainly Yogurt and Cheese
- Limited Red Meat and Sweets

Culinary Traditions:

Uncover the centuries-old culinary traditions that have shaped the Mediterranean diet. From Greek mezze to Italian antipasti, these appetizing customs reflect the region's cultural diversity and commitment to shared, joyful meals.

Key Ingredients and Flavors

Mediterranean Pantry Staples:

Embark on a journey through the Mediterranean pantry, discovering essential ingredients that impart the region's distinctive flavors to your dishes.

- *Olive Oil:* Liquid Gold of the Mediterranean
- *Herbs and Spices:* Oregano, Basil, Rosemary, and more
- *Citruses:* Lemons, Oranges, and Zesty Flavors
- *Legumes:* Chickpeas, Lentils, and Beans
- *Cheeses:* Feta, Mozzarella, and Pecorino

Flavorful Profiles:

Explore the harmonious blend of flavors that defines Mediterranean cuisine.

- *Balanced and Fresh:* A Symphony of Sweet, Salty, Bitter, and Sour
- *Citrus Zest:* Elevating Dishes with a Burst of Brightness
- *Herbaceous Delights:* Infusing Dishes with Fragrance and Depth

Health Benefits of Mediterranean Eating

Heart-Healthy Lifestyle:

Discover the science-backed benefits that make the Mediterranean diet a heart-healthy choice.

- *Rich in Omega-3 Fatty Acids:* Promoting Cardiovascular Health
- *Antioxidant-Rich Ingredients:* Combatting Inflammation
- *Low in Processed Foods:* Supporting Weight Management

Longevity and Well-Being:

Explore the link between Mediterranean eating and a longer, more vibrant life.

- *Mental Health:* Omega-3s and Brain Function
- *Reduced Risk of Chronic Diseases:* Diabetes, Cancer, and More
- *Enhanced Gut Health:* The Role of Fiber and Probiotics

Sustainable and Mindful Eating:

Understand how the Mediterranean diet promotes sustainable and mindful consumption.

- *Local and Seasonal Foods:* Reducing Environmental Impact
- *Moderation and Enjoyment:* Cultivating a Healthy Relationship with Food
- *Social and Culinary Joy:* The Pleasure of Shared Meals

By understanding the core principles, ingredients, flavors, and health benefits of the Mediterranean diet, you'll not only be mastering recipes but embracing a lifestyle that nurtures both body and soul

CHAPTER 2: GETTING STARTED WITH FREEZER MEALS

Equipment and Supplies

Essential Tools:

- *Quality Freezer Bags and Containers*: Ensure airtight seals to preserve freshness.
- *Vacuum Sealer:* Ideal for long-term storage and preventing freezer burn.
- *Labeling Tools:* Permanent markers and labels for easy identification.
- *Baking Sheets and Trays:* For flash-freezing individual portions.
- *Sharpie Knife or Kitchen Shears:* Efficiently cut and portion freezer-friendly ingredients.
- *Large Mixing Bowls:* For combining and marinating ingredients before freezing.

Optional, Yet Handy:

- *Slow Cooker or Instant Pot:* For easy, no-fuss cooking straight from the freezer.
- *Aluminum Foil and Parchment Paper:* Useful for creating protective layers to prevent freezer burn.
- *Silicone Ice Cube Trays:* Perfect for freezing small portions of sauces or herbs.

Essential Ingredients to Stock

Pantry Staples:

- *Quality Olive Oil:* A key ingredient for Mediterranean flavor.
- *Dried Herbs and Spices:* Oregano, Basil, Rosemary, Thyme, and more.
- *Canned Tomatoes and Tomato Paste:* Basis for many Mediterranean dishes.
- *Whole Grains:* Quinoa, Brown Rice, and Farro for nutritious bases.

Proteins:

- **Fish and Seafood:** Lean options like salmon, shrimp, and white fish.

- *Poultry:* Chicken and turkey, versatile and easy to portion.
- *Legumes:* Chickpeas, lentils, and various beans for plant-based protein.

Vegetables:

- *Leafy Greens:* Spinach, kale, and arugula for added nutrients.
- *Colorful Vegetables:* Bell peppers, tomatoes, zucchini, and eggplant.

Dairy and Cheese:

- **Greek Yogurt:** Versatile for both sweet and savory dishes.
- *Feta and Parmesan Cheese:* Add richness and depth to recipes.

Freezing Tips and Tricks

Batch Cooking Strategies:

- **Divide and Freeze:** Portion meals into smaller containers for easy reheating.

Flash-Freezing: Lay items flat on a baking sheet before transferring to bags for quick freezing.

Prevent Freezer Burn: Remove excess air from freezer bags, or use a vacuum sealer.

Smart Labeling:

- *Date and Contents:* Clearly label each package with the freezing date and meal details.
- *Cooking Instructions:* Include any additional steps or tips for reheating.

Proper Thawing Techniques:

- *Refrigerator Thawing:* Slow and controlled, ideal for most meals.
- *Cold-Water Bath:* Quick thawing for smaller items in sealed bags.
- *Direct Cooking from Frozen:* Suitable for certain recipes, such as casseroles or slow-cooker meals.

Refreshing Flavors After Freezing:

- *Fresh Herbs:* Add a burst of flavor by sprinkling fresh herbs on reheated dishes.

- *Lemon Zest:* Enhance brightness with a touch of citrus.
- *Finishing Touches:* Drizzle with quality olive oil or a squeeze of lemon before serving.

Armed with the right equipment, essential ingredients, and freezing know-how, you'll transform your kitchen into a freezer meal haven, ready to produce delightful Mediterranean dishes with ease.

CHAPTER 3: PLANNING AND PREPPING

Weekly Meal Planning Guide

Creating a Weekly Plan:

- *Assess Your Schedule:* Consider busy days and plan simpler meals.

- *Variety is Key:* Include a mix of proteins, grains, and vegetables.

- *Consider Themed Nights:* Embrace Mediterranean themes like "Greek Night" or "Italian Delights."

- *Mindful Portions:* Plan for leftovers to freeze for future meals.

Shopping List:

- *Check Pantry Staples:* Ensure you have essential Mediterranean ingredients.

- *Fresh Produce:* Purchase a variety of seasonal fruits and vegetables.

- *Proteins:* Include fish, poultry, legumes, and dairy in your list.
- *Freezer Containers and Bags:* Stock up on packaging materials.

Prep Day:

- *Chop and Prep Ingredients:* Spend a designated day chopping vegetables, marinating proteins, and preparing sauces.
- *Label Containers:* Label containers with the meal name and freezing date.
- *Organize the Freezer:* Allocate space for each day's meals for easy retrieval.

Batch Cooking Strategies

Cooking Efficiency:

- *Prepare Similar Ingredients Together:* Utilize shared ingredients for multiple recipes.
- *Utilize the Oven and Stovetop Simultaneously:* Maximize your cooking space.

- *Multi-Tasking:* While one dish is baking, work on the stovetop or prep the next recipe.

Portioning and Packaging:
- *Individual Portions:* Portion meals based on the number of people in your household.
- *Freezer Bags vs. Containers:* Consider the type of meal and storage space available.
- *Flash-Freezing:* Lay flat items like casseroles on a baking sheet for quicker freezing.

Smart Batch Cooking:
- *Protein Prep:* Cook large batches of proteins (chicken, fish) and portion for various recipes.
- *Versatile Base Ingredients:* Cook grains, pasta, and beans in bulk for multiple uses.

Freezer-Safe Containers and Packaging

Choosing the Right Containers:

- *Glass vs. Plastic:* Glass is ideal for reheating; plastic is lighter and may be more convenient for storage.
- *BPA-Free Containers:* Ensure containers are free from harmful chemicals.
- *Divided Containers:* Useful for separating main dishes and sides.

Packaging Tips:

- *Airtight Seals:* Prevent freezer burn by ensuring containers have secure, airtight seals.
- *Vacuum Sealing:* Ideal for preserving freshness and preventing ice crystals.
- *Labeling:* Clearly label containers with the meal name and freezing date.

Storage Tips:

- *Organized System:* Group similar meals together for easy access.
- *Rotate Stock:* Use the oldest meals first to maintain freshness.

- ***Maximize Freezer Space***: Efficiently stack containers to utilize space.

By following a weekly meal planning guide, implementing batch cooking strategies, and using proper freezer-safe containers, you'll streamline your meal preparation process and ensure a variety of delicious Mediterranean dishes at your fingertips whenever you need them.

CHAPTER 4: APPETIZERS AND SNACKS

1. Spanakopita Bites

Ingredients:

- Phyllo pastry sheets
- Fresh spinach
- Feta cheese
- Olive oil
- Garlic
- Nutmeg
- Salt and pepper

Instructions:

1. Sauté chopped garlic in olive oil until fragrant.

2. Add spinach and cook until wilted. Season with salt, pepper, and nutmeg.

3. Cut phyllo sheets into squares, fill with spinach mixture and feta, then fold into bite-sized triangles.

4. Bake until golden brown.

Nutritional Information (Per Serving):

- Calories: 120

- Protein: 5g
- Carbohydrates: 10g
- Fat: 7g
- Fiber: 1g
- Sugar: 1g
- Sodium: 180mg

2. Stuffed Grape Leaves (Dolma)

Ingredients:

- Grape leaves
- Rice
- Pine nuts
- Fresh dill
- Olive oil
- Lemon juice
- Salt and pepper

Instructions:

1. Mix cooked rice with pine nuts, chopped dill, olive oil, and lemon juice.

2. Place a spoonful of the mixture onto each grape leaf and roll tightly.

3. Steam or bake until grape leaves are tender.

Nutritional Information (Per Serving):

- Calories: 90
- Protein: 2g
- Carbohydrates: 15g
- Fat: 3g
- Fiber: 2g
- Sugar: 1g
- Sodium: 220mg

3. Mediterranean Hummus Cups

Ingredients:

- Mini phyllo cups
- Hummus
- Cherry tomatoes
- Kalamata olives
- Fresh parsley

Instructions:

1. Fill each phyllo cup with a spoonful of hummus.

2. Top with a halved cherry tomato and a slice of Kalamata olive.

3. Garnish with fresh parsley.

Nutritional Information (Per Serving):

- Calories: 100
- Protein: 3g
- Carbohydrates: 12g
- Fat: 5g
- Fiber: 3g
- Sugar: 1g
- Sodium: 160mg

4. Mozzarella and Tomato Skewers

Ingredients:

- Fresh mozzarella balls
- Cherry tomatoes
- Basil leaves
- Balsamic glaze
- Olive oil
- Salt and pepper

Instructions:

1. Thread a mozzarella ball, a folded basil leaf, and a cherry tomato onto small skewers.

2. Drizzle with olive oil and balsamic glaze.

3. Sprinkle with salt and pepper.

Nutritional Information (Per Serving):

- Calories: 80
- Protein: 4g
- Carbohydrates: 3g
- Fat: 6g
- Fiber: 1g
- Sugar: 1g
- Sodium: 120mg

5. Greek Yogurt and Cucumber Dip

Ingredients:

- Greek yogurt
- Cucumber
- Garlic
- Dill
- Lemon juice
- Olive oil
- Salt and pepper

Instructions:

1. Grate cucumber and squeeze out excess moisture.

2. Mix cucumber with Greek yogurt, minced garlic, chopped dill, lemon juice, and olive oil.

3. Season with salt and pepper.

Nutritional Information (Per Serving):

- Calories: 70
- Protein: 4g
- Carbohydrates: 5g
- Fat: 4g
- Fiber: 1g
- Sugar: 2g
- Sodium: 90mg

6. Roasted Red Pepper and Walnut Dip

Ingredients:

- Roasted red peppers
- Walnuts
- Garlic
- Olive oil

- Lemon juice
- Cumin
- Salt and pepper

Instructions:

1. Blend roasted red peppers, walnuts, minced garlic, olive oil, lemon juice, and cumin until smooth.

2. Season with salt and pepper.

Nutritional Information (Per Serving):

- Calories: 110
- Protein: 2g
- Carbohydrates: 4g
- Fat: 10g
- Fiber: 1g
- Sugar: 1g
- Sodium: 80mg

7. Mediterranean Bruschetta

Ingredients:

- Baguette slices
- Tomatoes
- Red onion

- Kalamata olives
- Feta cheese
- Fresh basil
- Balsamic glaze

Instructions:

1. Toast baguette slices.

2. Top with diced tomatoes, red onion, olives, and crumbled feta.

3. Garnish with fresh basil and drizzle with balsamic glaze.

Nutritional Information (Per Serving):

- Calories: 130
- Protein: 4g
- Carbohydrates: 18g
- Fat: 5g
- Fiber: 2g
- Sugar: 2g
- Sodium: 180mg

8. Chickpea and Roasted Garlic Dip

Ingredients:

- Chickpeas
- Roasted garlic
- Tahini
- Lemon juice
- Olive oil
- Cumin
- Salt and pepper

Instructions:

1. Blend chickpeas, roasted garlic, tahini, lemon juice, olive oil, and cumin until creamy.

2. Season with salt and pepper.

Nutritional Information (Per Serving):

- Calories: 90
- Protein: 3g
- Carbohydrates: 12g
- Fat: 4g
- Fiber: 3g
- Sugar: 1g
- Sodium: 120mg

9. Crispy Zucchini Fritters

Ingredients:

- Zucchini
- Feta cheese
- Eggs
- Flour
- Dill
- Garlic
- Olive oil
- Yogurt for dipping

Instructions:

1. Grate zucchini and squeeze out excess moisture.

2. Mix with crumbled feta, beaten eggs, flour, chopped dill, and minced garlic.

3. Fry in olive oil until golden brown.

Nutritional Information (Per Serving):

- Calories: 110
- Protein: 4g
- Carbohydrates: 8g
- Fat: 7g
- Fiber: 1g

- Sugar: 2g
- Sodium: 150mg

10. Olive and Herb Marinated Cheese

Ingredients:

- Cubes of your favorite cheese
- Assorted olives
- Fresh herbs (rosemary, thyme)
- Olive oil
- Lemon zest

Instructions:

1. Combine cheese cubes, olives, fresh herbs, and lemon zest in a bowl.

2. Drizzle with olive oil and toss gently.

3. Let marinate for at least 30 minutes before serving.

Nutritional Information (Per Serving):

- Calories: 150
- Protein: 6g
- Carbohydrates: 2g
- Fat: 13g

- Fiber: 1g
- Sugar: 0g
- Sodium: 220mg

Notes:

- Adjust serving sizes based on preferences and occasions.
- Encourage creativity by suggesting alternative ingredients or flavor variations.
- Remind readers to consider dietary restrictions and preferences when preparing these appetizers and snacks.

CHAPTER 5: MAIN COURSES

1. Chicken Souvlaki Skewers

Ingredients:

- Chicken breast, cubed
- Olive oil
- Lemon juice
- Garlic, minced
- Oregano
- Salt and pepper
- Cherry tomatoes and red onions for skewers

Instructions:

1. In a bowl, mix olive oil, lemon juice, minced garlic, oregano, salt, and pepper.

2. Marinate chicken cubes in the mixture for at least 30 minutes.

3. Thread chicken, cherry tomatoes, and red onions onto skewers.

4. Grill or bake until chicken is cooked through.

Nutritional Information (Per Serving):

- Calories: 250
- Protein: 25g

- Carbohydrates: 5g
- Fat: 15g
- Fiber: 1g
- Sugar: 2g
- Sodium: 300mg

2. Moussaka Casserole

Ingredients:

- Eggplant
- Ground lamb or beef
- Onion, diced
- Garlic, minced
- Tomato sauce
- Cinnamon
- Nutmeg
- Eggs
- Milk
- Parmesan cheese

Instructions:

1. Layer sliced and roasted eggplant at the bottom of a baking dish.

2. Sauté ground meat with onion and garlic, then add tomato sauce and spices.

3. Pour the meat mixture over the eggplant.

4. Whisk together eggs, milk, and Parmesan; pour over the casserole.

5. Bake until golden brown.

Nutritional Information (Per Serving):

- Calories: 350
- Protein: 20g
- Carbohydrates: 20g
- Fat: 22g
- Fiber: 4g
- Sugar: 8g
- Sodium: 400mg

3. Lemon Garlic Shrimp Pasta

Ingredients:

- Shrimp, peeled and deveined
- Linguine pasta
- Olive oil
- Garlic, minced

- Red pepper flakes
- Lemon juice and zest
- Fresh parsley
- Parmesan cheese

Instructions:

1. Cook pasta according to package instructions.

2. Sauté shrimp in olive oil with minced garlic and red pepper flakes.

3. Toss cooked pasta with shrimp, lemon juice, zest, and chopped parsley.

4. Serve with a sprinkle of Parmesan.

Nutritional Information (Per Serving):

- Calories: 300
- Protein: 25g
- Carbohydrates: 35g
- Fat: 10g
- Fiber: 2g
- Sugar: 2g
- Sodium: 200mg

4. Eggplant Parmesan Stacks

Ingredients:

- Eggplant slices
- Marinara sauce
- Mozzarella cheese
- Parmesan cheese
- Bread crumbs
- Fresh basil

Instructions:

1. Bread and bake eggplant slices until golden brown.

2. Layer eggplant with marinara sauce, mozzarella, and Parmesan.

3. Repeat to form stacks.

4. Bake until cheese is melted and bubbly.

5. Garnish with fresh basil.

Nutritional Information (Per Serving):

- Calories: 220
- Protein: 12g
- Carbohydrates: 15g
- Fat: 14g
- Fiber: 4g
- Sugar: 8g

- Sodium: 450mg

5. Lentil and Spinach Lasagna

Ingredients:

- Lasagna noodles
- Cooked lentils
- Spinach
- Ricotta cheese
- Marinara sauce
- Mozzarella cheese
- Garlic powder
- Italian seasoning

Instructions:

1. Cook lasagna noodles and layer in a baking dish.

2. Mix cooked lentils with spinach, ricotta, garlic powder, and Italian seasoning.

3. Layer lentil mixture, marinara sauce, and mozzarella.

4. Repeat and bake until bubbly.

Nutritional Information (Per Serving):

- Calories: 320
- Protein: 20g

- Carbohydrates: 40g
- Fat: 10g
- Fiber: 8g
- Sugar: 5g
- Sodium: 380mg

6. Chickpea and Spinach Stew

Ingredients:

- Chickpeas, cooked
- Spinach
- Onion, diced
- Tomatoes, diced
- Vegetable broth
- Cumin
- Paprika
- Lemon juice
- Fresh cilantro

Instructions:

1. Sauté onion until translucent; add cumin and paprika.

2. Add tomatoes, chickpeas, and vegetable broth; simmer.

3. Stir in fresh spinach until wilted.

4. Finish with lemon juice and cilantro.

Nutritional Information (Per Serving):

- Calories: 180
- Protein: 9g
- Carbohydrates: 30g
- Fat: 5g
- Fiber: 8g
- Sugar: 5g
- Sodium: 450mg

7. Vegetarian Paella

Ingredients:

- Arborio rice
- Vegetable broth
- Bell peppers
- Cherry tomatoes
- Artichoke hearts
- Saffron
- Smoked paprika
- White beans
- Lemon wedges

Instructions:

1. Sauté bell peppers and cherry tomatoes.

2. Add rice, saffron, and smoked paprika; stir.

3. Pour in vegetable broth and add artichoke hearts and white beans.

4. Simmer until rice is cooked.

5. Serve with lemon wedges.

Nutritional Information (Per Serving):

- Calories: 280
- Protein: 10g
- Carbohydrates: 50g
- Fat: 4g
- Fiber: 6g
- Sugar: 4g
- Sodium: 500mg

8. Lemon Herb Grilled Fish

Ingredients:

- White fish fillets
- Lemon juice and zest
- Fresh herbs (rosemary, thyme)

- Olive oil
- Garlic, minced
- Salt and pepper

Instructions:

1. Marinate fish in a mixture of lemon juice, zest, herbs, olive oil, minced garlic, salt, and pepper.

2. Grill until fish is flaky.

3. Garnish with extra herbs and a squeeze of lemon.

Nutritional Information (Per Serving):

- Calories: 200
- Protein: 25g
- Carbohydrates: 2g
- Fat: 10g
- Fiber: 1g
- Sugar: 0g
- Sodium: 300mg

Notes:

- Adjust servings based on individual needs.
- Encourage readers to customize recipes to suit personal tastes.

- Emphasize the versatility of these main courses, suitable for various occasions and dietary preferences.

CHAPTER 6: VEGETARIAN DELIGHTS

1. Mediterranean Quinoa Salad

Ingredients:

- Quinoa
- Cherry tomatoes, halved
- Cucumber, diced
- Kalamata olives, sliced
- Red onion, finely chopped
- Feta cheese, crumbled
- Fresh parsley, chopped
- Olive oil
- Lemon juice
- Salt and pepper

Instructions:

1. Cook quinoa according to package instructions.

2. In a large bowl, combine quinoa, tomatoes, cucumber, olives, red onion, and feta.

3. Drizzle with olive oil and lemon juice.

4. Season with salt and pepper, garnish with fresh parsley.

Nutritional Information (Per Serving):

- Calories: 280
- Protein: 10g
- Carbohydrates: 30g
- Fat: 15g
- Fiber: 5g
- Sugar: 2g
- Sodium: 400mg

2. Eggplant and Chickpea Curry

Ingredients:

- Eggplant, cubed
- Chickpeas, cooked
- Onion, diced
- Tomatoes, chopped
- Coconut milk
- Curry powder
- Cumin
- Coriander
- Garlic, minced
- Fresh cilantro, chopped

Instructions:

1. Sauté onion and garlic until softened.

2. Add eggplant, chickpeas, tomatoes, coconut milk, and spices.

3. Simmer until eggplant is tender.

4. Garnish with fresh cilantro.

Nutritional Information (Per Serving):

- Calories: 320
- Protein: 12g
- Carbohydrates: 40g
- Fat: 14g
- Fiber: 10g
- Sugar: 8g
- Sodium: 600mg

3. Caprese Stuffed Portobello Mushrooms

Ingredients:

- Portobello mushrooms
- Cherry tomatoes, sliced
- Fresh mozzarella, sliced

- Fresh basil leaves

Balsamic glaze

Olive oil

Salt and pepper

Instructions:

1. Remove stems from mushrooms and brush with olive oil.

2. Stuff with layers of tomatoes, mozzarella, and basil.

3. Drizzle with balsamic glaze, season with salt and pepper.

4. Bake until mushrooms are tender.

Nutritional Information (Per Serving):

- Calories: 180
- Protein: 12g
- Carbohydrates: 8g
- Fat: 12g
- Fiber: 2g
- Sugar: 4g
- Sodium: 250mg

4. Zucchini Noodles with Pesto

Ingredients:

- Zucchini, spiralized

- Cherry tomatoes, halved
- Pesto sauce (homemade or store-bought)
- Pine nuts, toasted
- Parmesan cheese, grated
- Fresh basil leaves
- Olive oil
- Salt and pepper

Instructions:

1. Sauté zucchini noodles in olive oil until tender.

2. Toss with cherry tomatoes, pesto, and pine nuts.

3. Garnish with grated Parmesan and fresh basil.

4. Season with salt and pepper.

Nutritional Information (Per Serving):

- Calories: 220
- Protein: 8g
- Carbohydrates: 10g
- Fat: 18g
- Fiber: 3g
- Sugar: 4g
- Sodium: 300mg

5. Mushroom and Spinach Stuffed Bell Peppers

Ingredients:

- Bell peppers, halved
- Mushrooms, diced
- Spinach, chopped
- Quinoa, cooked
- Feta cheese, crumbled
- Garlic, minced
- Olive oil
- Italian seasoning
- Salt and pepper

Instructions:

1. Roast bell peppers until slightly tender.

2. Sauté mushrooms, garlic, and spinach in olive oil.

3. Mix mushroom mixture with cooked quinoa and feta.

4. Stuff bell peppers, sprinkle with Italian seasoning.

5. Bake until peppers are fully cooked.

Nutritional Information (Per Serving):

- Calories: 250
- Protein: 12g

- Carbohydrates: 30g
- Fat: 10g
- Fiber: 7g
- Sugar: 5g
- Sodium: 350mg

6. Mediterranean Chickpea Salad

Ingredients:

- Chickpeas, cooked
- Cucumber, diced
- Cherry tomatoes, halved
- Red onion, finely chopped
- Feta cheese, crumbled
- Kalamata olives, sliced
- Fresh parsley, chopped
- Olive oil
- Lemon juice
- Garlic, minced
- Salt and pepper

Instructions:

1. Combine chickpeas, cucumber, tomatoes, red onion, feta, and olives.

2. In a separate bowl, whisk together olive oil, lemon juice, garlic, salt, and pepper.

3. Pour dressing over salad,

Nutritional Information (Per Serving):

- Calories: 280
- Protein: 10g
- Carbohydrates: 30g
- Fat: 15g
- Fiber: 5g
- Sugar: 2g
- Sodium: 400mg

7. Sweet Potato and Black Bean Enchiladas

Ingredients:

- Sweet potatoes, roasted and mashed
- Black beans, cooked
- Corn tortillas
- Enchilada sauce

- Red onion, diced
- Cilantro, chopped
- Avocado, sliced
- Lime wedges

Instructions:

1. Mix roasted sweet potatoes with black beans.

2. Spoon mixture into corn tortillas and roll.

3. Place in a baking dish, cover with enchilada sauce.

4. Bake until bubbly.

5. Garnish with red onion, cilantro, avocado, and lime.

Nutritional Information (Per Serving):

- Calories: 260
- Protein: 8g
- Carbohydrates: 40g
- Fat: 10g
- Fiber: 8g
- Sugar: 5g
- Sodium: 450mg

8. Spinach and Ricotta Stuffed Shells

Ingredients:

- Jumbo pasta shells
- Ricotta cheese
- Spinach, cooked and chopped
- Marinara sauce
- Mozzarella cheese, shredded
- Parmesan cheese, grated
- Fresh basil leaves

Instructions:

1. Cook pasta shells according to package instructions.

2. Mix ricotta with cooked spinach.

3. Stuff shells with the ricotta mixture.

4. Place in a baking dish, cover with marinara and cheeses.

5. Bake until cheese is melted and bubbly.

6. Garnish with fresh basil.

Nutritional Information (Per Serving):

- Calories: 300
- Protein: 15g
- Carbohydrates: 35g

- Fat: 12g
- Fiber: 5g
- Sugar: 8g
- Sodium: 400mg

9. Vegetarian Stir-Fry with Tofu

Ingredients:

- Firm tofu, cubed
- Mixed vegetables (broccoli, bell peppers, snap peas)
- Soy sauce
- Sesame oil
- Ginger, minced
- Garlic, minced
- Green onions, chopped
- Brown rice, cooked

Instructions:

1. Sauté tofu until golden brown.

2. Add mixed vegetables, ginger, and garlic.

3. Stir in soy sauce and sesame oil.

4. Cook until vegetables are tender.

5. Serve over cooked brown rice.

6. Garnish with chopped green onions.

Nutritional Information (Per Serving):

- Calories: 280
- Protein: 18g
- Carbohydrates: 30g
- Fat: 10g
- Fiber: 6g
- Sugar: 4g
- Sodium: 600mg

10. Butternut Squash and Sage Risotto

Ingredients:

- Arborio rice
- Butternut squash, diced and roasted
- Vegetable broth
- White wine
- Onion, finely chopped
- Fresh sage leaves, chopped
- Parmesan cheese, grated
- Butter

- Salt and pepper

Instructions:

1. Sauté onion in butter until translucent.

2. Add Arborio rice and cook until lightly toasted.

3. Pour in white wine and cook until evaporated.

4. Gradually add vegetable broth, stirring continuously.

5. Stir in roasted butternut squash and sage.

6. Continue cooking until rice is creamy.

7. Finish with grated Parmesan, salt, and pepper.

Nutritional Information (Per Serving):

- Calories: 320
- Protein: 8g
- Carbohydrates: 55g
- Fat: 8g
- Fiber: 6g
- Sugar: 4g
- Sodium: 500mg

Notes:

- Adjust servings based on individual needs.
- Encourage readers to customize recipes to suit personal tastes.

- Highlight the nutritional benefits of each dish, emphasizing the variety of nutrients present in a vegetarian diet.

CHAPTER 7: SIDE DISHES

1. Roasted Garlic and Herb Potatoes

Ingredients:

- Potatoes, cubed
- Olive oil
- Garlic, minced
- Fresh rosemary, chopped
- Fresh thyme leaves
- Salt and pepper

Instructions:

1. Toss potatoes with olive oil, minced garlic, rosemary, and thyme.

2. Spread on a baking sheet and roast until golden brown.

3. Season with salt and pepper.

Nutritional Information (Per Serving):

- Calories: 180
- Protein: 3g
- Carbohydrates: 30g
- Fat: 6g

- Fiber: 4g
- Sugar: 2g
- Sodium: 250mg

2. Grilled Asparagus with Lemon Zest

Ingredients:

- Fresh asparagus spears
- Olive oil
- Lemon zest
- Salt and pepper

Instructions:

1. Trim asparagus and toss with olive oil.

2. Grill until tender and slightly charred.

3. Sprinkle with lemon zest.

4. Season with salt and pepper.

Nutritional Information (Per Serving):

- Calories: 40
- Protein: 2g
- Carbohydrates: 5g
- Fat: 3g

- Fiber: 3g
- Sugar: 2g
- Sodium: 150mg

3. Quinoa and Black Bean Stuffed Peppers

Ingredients:

- Bell peppers, halved
- Quinoa, cooked
- Black beans, cooked
- Corn kernels
- Red onion, diced
- Cilantro, chopped
- Lime juice
- Cumin
- Salt and pepper

Instructions:

1. Combine cooked quinoa, black beans, corn, red onion, and cilantro.

2. Squeeze lime juice over the mixture and add cumin, salt, and pepper.

3. Stuff bell pepper halves with the mixture.

Nutritional Information (Per Serving):

- Calories: 160
- Protein: 6g
- Carbohydrates: 30g
- Fat: 2g
- Fiber: 6g
- Sugar: 3g
- Sodium: 300mg

4. Crispy Brussels Sprouts with Balsamic Glaze

Ingredients:

- Brussels sprouts, halved
- Olive oil
- Balsamic glaze
- Garlic powder
- Salt and pepper

Instructions:

1. Toss Brussels sprouts with olive oil and garlic powder.

2. Roast until crispy and golden.

3. Drizzle with balsamic glaze.

4. Season with salt and pepper.

Nutritional Information (Per Serving):

- Calories: 90
- Protein: 4g
- Carbohydrates: 12g
- Fat: 4g
- Fiber: 4g
- Sugar: 3g
- Sodium: 120mg

5. Lemon Herb Quinoa

Ingredients:

- Quinoa, cooked
- Lemon zest
- Fresh parsley, chopped
- Fresh dill, chopped
- Olive oil
- Salt and pepper

Instructions:

1. Fluff cooked quinoa with a fork.

2. Mix in lemon zest, parsley, and dill.

3. Drizzle with olive oil.

4. Season with salt and pepper.

Nutritional Information (Per Serving):

- Calories: 160
- Protein: 5g
- Carbohydrates: 25g
- Fat: 5g
- Fiber: 3g
- Sugar: 1g
- Sodium: 200mg

6. Mediterranean Couscous Salad

Ingredients:

- Couscous, cooked
- Cherry tomatoes, halved
- Cucumber, diced
- Kalamata olives, sliced
- Red onion, finely chopped
- Feta cheese, crumbled
- Fresh mint leaves, chopped

- Olive oil
- Lemon juice
- Salt and pepper

Instructions:

1. Combine cooked couscous, tomatoes, cucumber, olives, red onion, feta, and mint.

2. Drizzle with olive oil and lemon juice.

3. Season with salt and pepper.

Nutritional Information (Per Serving):

- Calories: 220
- Protein: 7g
- Carbohydrates: 35g
- Fat: 7g
- Fiber: 5g
- Sugar: 2g
- Sodium: 300mg

7. Garlic Parmesan Roasted Broccoli

Ingredients:

- Broccoli florets

- Olive oil
- Garlic, minced
- Parmesan cheese, grated
- Lemon juice
- Salt and pepper

Instructions:

1. Toss broccoli with olive oil and minced garlic.

2. Roast until crisp-tender.

3. Sprinkle with Parmesan and drizzle with lemon juice.

4. Season with salt and pepper.

Nutritional Information (Per Serving):

- Calories: 70
- Protein: 5g
- Carbohydrates: 8g
- Fat: 3g
- Fiber: 3g
- Sugar: 2g
- Sodium: 120mg

8. Baked Stuffed Artichokes

Ingredients:

- Artichokes, halved
- Bread crumbs
- Parmesan cheese, grated
- Garlic, minced
- Lemon zest
- Olive oil
- Fresh parsley, chopped
- Salt and pepper

Instructions:

1. Mix bread crumbs, Parmesan, garlic, lemon zest, and parsley.

2. Stuff artichoke halves with the mixture.

3. Drizzle with olive oil.

4. Bake until artichokes are tender.

Nutritional Information (Per Serving):

- Calories: 120
- Protein: 4g
- Carbohydrates: 15g
- Fat: 6g
- Fiber: 6g
- Sugar: 2g
- Sodium: 250mg

9. Herbed Wild Rice Pilaf

Ingredients:

- Wild rice, cooked
- Fresh thyme leaves
- Rosemary, chopped
- Pecans, toasted and chopped
- Dried cranberries
- Olive oil
- Orange zest
- Salt and pepper

Instructions:

1. Combine cooked wild rice, thyme, rosemary, pecans, and cranberries.

2. Drizzle with olive oil and toss.

3. Garnish with orange zest.

4. Season with salt and pepper.

Nutritional Information (Per Serving):

- Calories: 180
- Protein: 5g
- Carbohydrates: 25g

- Fat: 8g
- Fiber: 4g
- Sugar: 4g
- Sodium: 150mg

10. Sweet and Savory Roasted Butternut Squash

Ingredients:

- Butternut squash, peeled and cubed
- Maple syrup
- Balsamic vinegar
- Fresh thyme leaves
- Olive oil
- Salt and pepper

Instructions:

1. Toss butternut squash with maple syrup, balsamic vinegar, and thyme.

2. Drizzle with olive oil and toss to coat.

3. Roast until caramelized.

4. Season with salt and pepper.

Nutritional Information (Per Serving):

- Calories: 120
- Protein: 2g
- Carbohydrates: 30g
- Fat: 3g
- Fiber: 5g
- Sugar: 10g
- Sodium: 150mg

Notes:

- Adjust servings based on individual needs.
- Encourage readers to experiment with different herbs and spices for added flavor.
- Emphasize the versatility of these side dishes, perfect for complementing any Mediterranean-inspired meal.

CHAPTER 8: SAUCES AND CONDIMENTS

1. Tzatziki Sauce

Ingredients:

- Greek yogurt
- Cucumber, finely diced
- Garlic, minced
- Fresh dill, chopped
- Lemon juice
- Olive oil
- Salt and pepper

Instructions:

1. In a bowl, combine Greek yogurt, cucumber, garlic, and dill.

2. Stir in lemon juice and olive oil.

3. Season with salt and pepper to taste.

Nutritional Information (Per Serving):

- Calories: 60
- Protein: 3g
- Carbohydrates: 5g

- Fat: 3g
- Fiber: 1g
- Sugar: 3g
- Sodium: 40mg

2. Classic Pesto Sauce

Ingredients:

- Fresh basil leaves
- Pine nuts, toasted
- Parmesan cheese, grated
- Garlic, minced
- Olive oil
- Lemon juice
- Salt and pepper

Instructions:

1. Blend basil, pine nuts, Parmesan, and garlic in a food processor.

2. Gradually add olive oil and lemon juice while blending.

3. Season with salt and pepper to taste.

Nutritional Information (Per Serving):

- Calories: 120

- Protein: 3g
- Carbohydrates: 3g
- Fat: 12g
- Fiber: 1g
- Sugar: 0g
- Sodium: 150mg

3. Roasted Red Pepper Hummus

Ingredients:

- Chickpeas, canned
- Roasted red peppers
- Tahini
- Garlic, minced
- Lemon juice
- Olive oil
- Cumin
- Paprika
- Salt and pepper

Instructions:

1. Blend chickpeas, roasted red peppers, tahini, and garlic in a food processor.

2. Add lemon juice, olive oil, cumin, and paprika.

3. Season with salt and pepper to taste.

Nutritional Information (Per Serving):

- Calories: 100
- Protein: 4g
- Carbohydrates: 12g
- Fat: 5g
- Fiber: 3g
- Sugar: 2g
- Sodium: 180mg

4. Lemon Garlic Aioli

Ingredients:

- Mayonnaise
- Garlic, minced
- Lemon zest
- Lemon juice
- Dijon mustard
- Olive oil
- Salt and pepper

Instructions:

1. Whisk together mayonnaise, minced garlic, lemon zest, and lemon juice.

2. Stir in Dijon mustard.

3. Gradually add olive oil while whisking.

4. Season with salt and pepper to taste.

Nutritional Information (Per Serving):

- Calories: 90
- Protein: 0g
- Carbohydrates: 1g
- Fat: 10g
- Fiber: 0g
- Sugar: 0g
- Sodium: 80mg

5. Balsamic Glaze

Ingredients:

- Balsamic vinegar
- Honey
- Soy sauce (optional)

Instructions:

1. In a saucepan, combine balsamic vinegar and honey.

2. Bring to a simmer and cook until it thickens.

3. Add soy sauce for extra depth if desired.

4. Let it cool before serving.

Nutritional Information (Per Serving):

- Calories: 40
- Protein: 0g
- Carbohydrates: 10g
- Fat: 0g
- Fiber: 0g
- Sugar: 9g
- Sodium: 10mg

6. Olive Tapenade

Ingredients:

- Kalamata olives, pitted
- Capers
- Garlic, minced
- Fresh parsley, chopped
- Lemon juice
- Olive oil

- Black pepper

Instructions:

1. Blend olives, capers, garlic, and parsley in a food processor.

2. Add lemon juice and olive oil.

3. Pulse until desired consistency.

4. Season with black pepper to taste.

Nutritional Information (Per Serving):

- Calories: 80
- Protein: 1g
- Carbohydrates: 3g
- Fat: 8g
- Fiber: 1g
- Sugar: 0g
- Sodium: 450mg

7. Sundried Tomato Pesto

Ingredients:

- Sundried tomatoes, packed in oil
- Fresh basil leaves
- Pine nuts, toasted

- Parmesan cheese, grated
- Garlic, minced
- Olive oil
- Lemon juice
- Salt and pepper

Instructions:

1. Blend sundried tomatoes, basil, pine nuts, Parmesan, and garlic in a food processor.

2. Gradually add olive oil and lemon juice while blending.

3. Season with salt and pepper to taste.

Nutritional Information (Per Serving):

- Calories: 120
- Protein: 3g
- Carbohydrates: 5g
- Fat: 12g
- Fiber: 2g
- Sugar: 2g
- Sodium: 180mg

8. Greek Salad Dressing

Ingredients:

- Olive oil
- Red wine vinegar
- Dijon mustard
- Garlic, minced
- Oregano
- Salt and pepper

Instructions:

1. Whisk together olive oil, red wine vinegar, Dijon mustard, and minced garlic.

2. Stir in oregano.

3. Season with salt and pepper to taste.

Nutritional Information (Per Serving):

- Calories: 80
- Protein: 0g
- Carbohydrates: 1g
- Fat: 9g
- Fiber: 0g
- Sugar: 0g
- Sodium: 80mg

9. **Cilantro Lime Crema**

Ingredients:

- Sour cream or Greek yogurt
- Fresh cilantro, chopped
- Lime zest
- Lime juice
- Garlic, minced
- Salt and pepper

Instructions:

1. Mix sour cream or Greek yogurt with chopped cilantro, lime zest, and lime juice.

2. Stir in minced garlic.

3. Season with salt and pepper to taste.

Nutritional Information (Per Serving):

- Calories: 60
- Protein: 1g
- Carbohydrates: 2g
- Fat: 6g
- Fiber: 0g
- Sugar: 1g
- Sodium: 20mg

10. Mango Salsa

Ingredients:

- Mango, diced
- Red onion, finely chopped
- Jalapeño, minced
- Fresh cilantro, chopped
- Lime juice
- Salt and pepper

Instructions:

1. Combine diced mango, red onion, jalapeño, and cilantro in a bowl.

2. Drizzle with lime juice.

3. Season with salt and pepper to taste.

Nutritional Information (Per Serving):

- Calories: 40
- Protein: 0g
- Carbohydrates: 10g
- Fat: 0g
- Fiber: 1g
- Sugar: 8g
- Sodium: 0mg

Notes:

- Adjust servings based on individual needs.
- Encourage readers to store these sauces and condiments in airtight containers for freshness.
- Mention the versatility of these condiments, suitable for various Mediterranean dishes.

CHAPTER 9: SWEET TREATS

1. Mediterranean Orange and Almond Cake

Ingredients:

- Almond flour
- Eggs
- Honey
- Orange zest
- Baking powder
- Salt

Instructions:

1. Preheat the oven and grease a cake pan.

2. Mix almond flour, eggs, honey, orange zest, baking powder, and a pinch of salt.

3. Pour the batter into the pan and bake until golden.

4. Allow to cool before slicing.

Nutritional Information (Per Serving):

- Calories: 180
- Protein: 6g
- Carbohydrates: 15g

- Fat: 12g
- Fiber: 3g
- Sugar: 10g
- Sodium: 80mg

2. Greek Yogurt and Honey Parfait

Ingredients:

- Greek yogurt
- Honey
- Fresh berries
- Granola

Instructions:

1. In a glass, layer Greek yogurt, honey, fresh berries, and granola.

2. Repeat the layers until the glass is filled.

3. Serve immediately and enjoy!

Nutritional Information (Per Serving):

- Calories: 220
- Protein: 15g
- Carbohydrates: 30g
- Fat: 6g

- Fiber: 5g
- Sugar: 15g
- Sodium: 40mg

3. Date and Nut Energy Bites

Ingredients:

- Dates, pitted
- Almonds
- Walnuts
- Chia seeds
- Coconut flakes

Instructions:

1. In a food processor, blend dates, almonds, and walnuts until a sticky mixture forms.

2. Add chia seeds and pulse until combined.

3. Roll into bite-sized balls and coat with coconut flakes.

4. Refrigerate before serving.

Nutritional Information (Per Serving - 2 Bites):

- Calories: 120
- Protein: 3g
- Carbohydrates: 15g

- Fat: 6g
- Fiber: 4g
- Sugar: 10g
- Sodium: 0mg

4. Pistachio and Honey Baklava Bars

Ingredients:

- Phyllo dough
- Pistachios, chopped
- Butter, melted
- Honey
- Cinnamon

Instructions:

1. Preheat the oven and layer phyllo dough, brushing each layer with melted butter.

2. Sprinkle chopped pistachios and cinnamon between the layers.

3. Bake until golden brown and cut into bars.

4. Drizzle honey over the top before serving.

Nutritional Information (Per Serving):

- Calories: 200
- Protein: 4g
- Carbohydrates: 20g
- Fat: 12g
- Fiber: 2g
- Sugar: 8g
- Sodium: 90mg

5. Mediterranean Yogurt and Fig Popsicles

Ingredients:
- Greek yogurt
- Fresh figs, diced
- Honey
- Vanilla extract

Instructions:

1. In a bowl, mix Greek yogurt, diced figs, honey, and vanilla extract.

2. Pour the mixture into popsicle molds.

3. Freeze until solid and enjoy on a hot day!

Nutritional Information (Per Popsicle):

- Calories: 80
- Protein: 5g
- Carbohydrates: 10g
- Fat: 3g
- Fiber: 1g
- Sugar: 8g
- Sodium: 20mg

6. Olive Oil and Orange Polenta Cake

Ingredients:

- Polenta
- Almond flour
- Olive oil
- Eggs
- Orange juice
- Baking powder
- Orange zest

Instructions:

1. Mix polenta, almond flour, olive oil, eggs, orange juice, baking powder, and orange zest.

2. Pour into a cake pan and bake until a toothpick comes out clean.

3. Allow to cool before slicing.

Nutritional Information (Per Serving):

- Calories: 220
- Protein: 6g
- Carbohydrates: 20g
- Fat: 14g
- Fiber: 3g
- Sugar: 8g
- Sodium: 70mg

7. Mediterranean Fruit Salad

Ingredients:

- Watermelon, cubed
- Feta cheese, crumbled
- Mint leaves, chopped
- Balsamic glaze

Instructions:

1. In a large bowl, combine cubed watermelon, crumbled feta, and chopped mint.

2. Drizzle with balsamic glaze before serving.

Nutritional Information (Per Serving):

- Calories: 120
- Protein: 4g
- Carbohydrates: 20g
- Fat: 4g
- Fiber: 2g
- Sugar: 16g
- Sodium: 180mg

8. Almond and Honey Phyllo Cups

Ingredients:

- Mini phyllo cups
- Almond butter
- Honey
- Sliced almonds

Instructions:

1. Fill mini phyllo cups with almond butter.

2. Drizzle honey over the top and sprinkle with sliced almonds.

3. Serve as a delightful bite-sized dessert.

Nutritional Information (Per Serving - 2 Cups):

- Calories: 100
- Protein: 3g
- Carbohydrates: 12g
- Fat: 5g
- Fiber: 1g
- Sugar: 5g
- Sodium: 40mg

9. Greek Yogurt and Lemon Mousse

Ingredients:

- Greek yogurt
- Lemon juice
- Lemon zest
- Honey
- Whipped cream (optional)

Instructions:

1. In a bowl, mix Greek yogurt, lemon juice, lemon zest, and honey.

2. If desired, fold in whipped cream for a lighter texture.

3. Chill in the refrigerator before serving.

Nutritional Information (Per Serving):

- Calories: 150
- Protein: 8g
- Carbohydrates: 20g
- Fat: 5g
- Fiber: 1g
- Sugar: 18g
- Sodium: 20mg

10. Chocolate and Olive Oil Mousse

Ingredients:

- Dark chocolate, melted
- Olive oil
- Eggs, separated
- Sugar
- Vanilla extract
- Sea salt

Instructions:

1. Melt dark chocolate and mix with olive oil.

2. In a separate bowl, beat egg yolks with sugar and vanilla extract.

3. Combine chocolate mixture with egg yolk mixture.

4. In another bowl, whip egg whites until stiff peaks form.

5. Gently fold egg whites into the chocolate mixture.

6. Chill in the refrigerator before serving.

Nutritional Information (Per Serving):

- Calories: 180
- Protein: 4g
- Carbohydrates: 15g
- Fat: 12g
- Fiber: 2g
- Sugar: 12g
- Sodium: 30mg

Notes:

- Adjust servings based on individual needs.
- Suggest serving sizes to help with portion control.
- Encourage readers to experiment with different fruits and nuts for added variety in the sweet treats.

CHAPTER 10: TIPS FOR SUCCESS

1. Proper Thawing Techniques

a. Refrigerator Thawing:

- Place the frozen meal in the refrigerator 24 to 48 hours before cooking.
- Ensure the meal is in an airtight container or securely wrapped to prevent cross-contamination.
- Thawing in the refrigerator maintains the quality and safety of the ingredients.

b. Cold Water Thawing:

- Submerge the sealed freezer meal in a leak-proof plastic bag.
- Change the water every 30 minutes to maintain a safe temperature.
- Thawing times vary based on the meal size but are generally faster than refrigerator thawing.

c. Microwave Thawing:

- Use the defrost function on the microwave, following the appliance's guidelines.

- Thawing in the microwave is suitable for smaller portions but may affect texture and quality.

2. Adjusting Cooking Times for Freezer Meals

a. Oven-Baked Meals:

- Increase the cooking time by 15-30 minutes for frozen casseroles and baked dishes.
- Cover with foil for part of the cooking time to prevent excessive browning.

b. Slow Cooker Meals:

- Add 1-2 hours to the cooking time for frozen slow cooker meals.
- Ensure that the internal temperature reaches a safe level for all ingredients.

c. Stovetop Cooking:

- Allow extra time for thawed ingredients to come to room temperature before cooking.
- Adjust cooking times based on the density of frozen ingredients.

3. Refreshing Flavors After Freezing

a. Herb and Spice Boost:

- Add fresh herbs or a dash of spices during the reheating process to enhance flavor.
- Experiment with aromatic herbs like basil, cilantro, or thyme to elevate the dish.

b. Citrus Zest and Juice:

- Squeeze fresh lemon or lime juice over frozen meals to brighten flavors.
- Grate citrus zest for a burst of freshness, especially effective in Mediterranean dishes.

c. Finish with Fresh Ingredients:

- Top reheated meals with fresh ingredients like chopped tomatoes, avocado, or a handful of greens.
- Crumbled feta or grated Parmesan adds a savory kick to many Mediterranean dishes.

d. Customized Sauces:

- Drizzle a light, complementary sauce over frozen meals before serving.

- Experiment with homemade tzatziki, pesto, or a balsamic glaze for added depth.

e. Crunchy Toppings:

- Toast nuts or seeds separately and sprinkle over frozen dishes before serving.
- Crispy elements add texture and contrast to reheated freezer meals.

4. Safety Reminders:

- Always follow safe food handling guidelines.
- Discard any frozen meal that has been left at room temperature for more than 2 hours.
- Use a food thermometer to ensure internal temperatures meet recommended levels.

Note:

Encourage readers to use these techniques thoughtfully and consider the specific ingredients and cooking methods used in each recipe. Tailoring the adjustments based on the type of dish and personal preferences will contribute to a successful and flavorful dining experience.

CONCLUSION

As we reach the end of this Mediterranean Freezer Meals Cookbook, we hope to have equipped you with a treasure trove of delicious and convenient recipes that not only embrace the richness of the Mediterranean diet but also make your daily culinary journey a delightful experience. This cookbook isn't just about freezing meals; it's about savoring the essence of Mediterranean flavors at your convenience.

From the aromatic herbs of Greece to the hearty grains of Italy, each recipe has been crafted to bring the warmth of the Mediterranean right to your table. The freezer-friendly nature of these meals ensures that your busy lifestyle doesn't compromise on the quality and nutrition of your food.

In addition to the mouthwatering recipes, we've provided you with essential tips and techniques for proper meal preparation, thawing, and refreshing flavors after freezing. Whether you're a seasoned chef or just starting your culinary adventure, we believe this cookbook will inspire and simplify your meal planning.

Remember, the heart of the Mediterranean diet lies not only in the ingredients but in the joy of sharing wholesome, flavorful meals with loved ones. So, gather your family and friends, dive into the world of Mediterranean cuisine, and enjoy the convenience of freezer meals without compromising on taste and nutrition.

Cook with passion, savor with pleasure, and let the Mediterranean flavors elevate your everyday dining experience.

Happy cooking!

APPENDIX

Bonus Section: Conversion Charts and Ingredient Substitution Guide

Conversion Charts:

1. Volume Conversions:

- 1 cup = 16 tablespoons
- 1 tablespoon = 3 teaspoons
- 1 fluid ounce = 2 tablespoons

2. Weight Conversions:

- 1 ounce = 28 grams
- 1 pound = 16 ounces
- 1 kilogram = 2.2 pounds

3. Temperature Conversions:

- Fahrenheit to Celsius: °F - 32°F−32 × 5/95/9
- Celsius to Fahrenheit: °C × 9/5°C×9/5 + 32

4. Common Oven Temperature Equivalents:

- Moderate oven: 350°F (180°C)

- Moderate to hot oven: 375°F (190°C)
- Hot oven: 400°F (200°C)
- Very hot oven: 425°F (220°C)
- Extremely hot oven: 450°F (230°C)

Ingredient Substitution Guide:

1. Flour:

- All-purpose flour can usually be substituted with whole wheat flour in many recipes.
- Gluten-free flour blends are a great alternative for those with gluten sensitivity.

2. Sugar:

- White sugar can often be replaced with brown sugar or vice versa.
- Honey or maple syrup can be used as a natural sweetener instead of granulated sugar.

3. Butter:

- In baking, coconut oil or vegetable oil can be used as a substitute for butter.

- Applesauce or mashed bananas work well in some recipes as a butter alternative.

4. Milk:

- Dairy-free milk alternatives such as almond, soy, or oat milk can replace regular milk.
- Yogurt or buttermilk can often be used in place of milk in recipes.

5. Eggs:

- In baking, applesauce, mashed bananas, or yogurt can replace eggs.
- Silken tofu or commercial egg replacers are suitable for some recipes.

6. Olive Oil:

- Canola oil, vegetable oil, or avocado oil are good substitutes for olive oil in cooking.
- For dressings, nut oils like walnut or almond oil can add a unique flavor.

7. Herbs and Spices:

- Dried herbs can generally be replaced with fresh herbs, and vice versa.
- Experiment with different herbs and spices to tailor the flavor to your preference.

8. Cheese:

- For a dairy-free option, nutritional yeast can provide a cheesy flavor in some recipes.
- Goat cheese or feta can often be interchangeable in Mediterranean dishes.

9. Nuts:

- Different nuts can often be substituted for each other in recipes.
- Sunflower seeds or pumpkin seeds can be used as nut alternatives for added crunch.

10. Tomato Sauce:

- Tomato paste diluted with water or broth can replace tomato sauce.
- Crushed tomatoes or diced tomatoes blended can be used in place of tomato sauce.

Remember, the key to successful substitutions is understanding the role of the ingredient in the recipe and choosing a substitute with similar properties. Feel free to get creative and tailor recipes to your taste preferences and dietary needs.

Made in United States
Cleveland, OH
18 December 2024

12178211R00059